# CHRIS EVERT
## PRINCESS OF TENNIS

# CHRIS EVERT
## PRINCESS OF TENNIS

## by Julian May

Published by Crestwood House, Inc., Mankato, Minnesota 56001. Text copyright © 1975 by Julian May Dikty. Illustrations copyright © 1975 by Crestwood House, Inc. All rights reserved. No part of this book may be reproduced in any form without written permission from the publisher, except for brief passages included in a review. Printed in the United States of America.

Reprinted 1978

Designed by William Dichtl                                          Revised 1977

Library of Congress Catalog Card Number: 75-28936

International Standard Book Numbers: ` 
0-913940-35-6 Library Bound
0-89686-001-9 Paperback

**Crestwood House, Inc., Mankato, Minn. 56001**

## PHOTO CREDITS

# CHRIS EVERT
## PRINCESS OF TENNIS

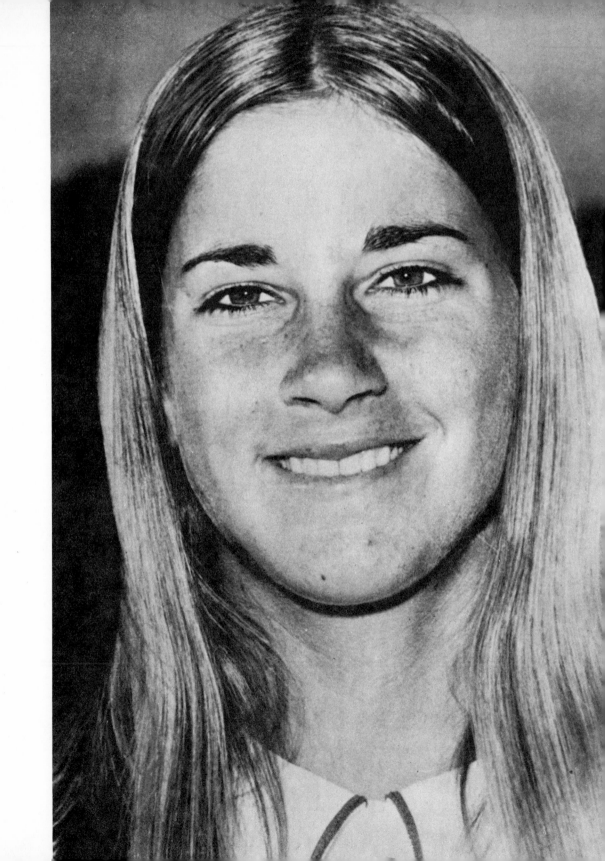

The little six-year-old blonde girl gripped the tennis racket. She stared solemnly at her father.

He said: "Chrissie, today you're going to learn to play Daddy's game."

Christine Marie Evert nodded. Her father, Jimmy Evert, gently threw a ball over the net to her.

She swung hard! She missed.

Again and again Jimmy Evert threw the ball to his daughter. She missed every time. But he said: "That's a good start, Chrissie. We'll try again tomorrow."

For many weeks after that, Jimmy Evert threw balls for his little girl. After she learned to hit, he would shout:

"Ten over the net and I'll buy you a Coke!"

She would hit the ball without smiling, thinking only of what she was doing. "I'm going to learn to play Daddy's game *good*," said little Christine Evert.

And she did.

Chris Evert with her family, in a photo taken when Chris was 17. In the front row *(from left):* brother John, Mrs. Colette Evert, sister Jeanne, Jimmy Evert. In the rear are brother Drew and little sister Clare.

When he was a young man, Jimmy Evert had played in tennis tournaments. He had won the National Indoor Junior title. He was captain of the tennis team at Notre Dame. Later, he became a tennis pro in Fort Lauderdale, Florida. He was in charge of the city's tennis program and taught people to play the game.

The Evert house was just six blocks away from the courts where Jimmy Evert worked. The five Evert children (Christine was the second) all learned to play their Daddy's game. They all loved it.

8

Chris took tennis more seriously than most of the other Evert children. When she was seven, she practiced four hours every weekday and nine hours on weekends. One Christmas day, her aunt telephoned the family. She wanted to say hello to Chris—but she couldn't. The girl was out on the tennis court, practicing!

When she was eight, Chris and another girl were runners up in a doubles tournament at the Orange Bowl. They won a trophy. It made Chris very happy.

When she was a little older, she competed in national tournaments. She was a nationally ranked player at 11 and began to win.

In 1968, Chris won the National Girls' 14, her first junior championship. In 1970 she won the Girls' 16, and in 1971 she won the Girls' 18 and the Orange Bowl.

Chris went to St. Thomas Aquinas Catholic High School in Fort Lauderdale. She got good grades, but she didn't spend much time doing the things the other kids did. After school, Chris went right out on the court. She and her younger sister, Jeanne, would practice for hours.

Chris had boy friends and went on dates, but she soon learned not to go out with boys who played tennis. When she beat them, their feelings would be hurt. Then goodbye!

Chris *(front)* with her classmates at St. Thomas Aquinas High School.

Chris practiced hard before the Wightman Cup matches in 1971.

Tennis became more and more important to Chris. She developed great control, but she lacked a strong backhand. So her father taught her to hit the shot holding the racket in both hands. It was weird, but it worked! Chris played better and better.

In 1970, when she was 15, she went to a tournament at Charlotte, N.C. There she beat a high-ranked woman, Francoise Durr of France. The next day, she defeated Margaret Smith Court, who had won at Wimbledon that year!

When it was all over, Chris Evert burst into tears.

She made steady progress. In the spring of 1971, she played in the Virginia Slims Masters and beat Billie Jean King. She could not accept the winner's purse in that contest because she was still an amateur.

Chris Evert was invited to play on the U.S. women's Wightman Cup team. The contest, between England and the United States, is always hotly fought. At 16, Chris was the youngest player to be selected for the team since Maureen Connolly in 1951. (The beloved "Little Mo" Connolly was 16, too. She went on to win three Wimbledons in a row in 1952, 1953, and 1954.)

Many people thought that Chris's game was still too weak for important competitions. But she played coolly and well at the Wightman matches. Finally, it all came down to Chris Evert of the U.S. versus Virginia Wade of England. The winner would take home the Cup for her country.

Virginia Wade was England's best woman player. But Chris waded in and demolished her, 6-1, 6-1. The United States won the Wightman Cup, and the tennis world sat up and took notice of Christine Marie Evert.

Chris displays the form she used to beat England's top woman player, Virginia Wade, in the 1971 Wightman matches.

She was young and pretty and talented. She became the pet of the fans and the sportswriters. At the U.S. Open at Forest Hills that fall, huge crowds watched her play.

In the first round, Chris beat Edda Budding of Germany, 6-1, 6-0. The next day, Chris faced a more powerful rival, Mary Ann Eisel, ranked No. 4 in the United States. Chris lost the first set, then bounced back to win both the second set and the tie-breaker.

14          Chris goes after Germany's Edda Budding at Forest Hills in 1971.

Then Chris played Francoise Durr. The crowd was clearly on the side of the blonde American. When Chris lost the first set, everybody groaned.

Once again, Chris pulled it out of the fire. She defeated Durr in the second set, 6-2, then won the third set, 6-3. As she shook hands with the defeated Frenchwoman, the entire audience stood up and cheered.

Francoise Durr, French tennis star, congratulates Chris after their Forest Hills match.

In the quarter-finals, Chris faced Lesley Hunt of Australia. Since the crowd was so obviously on Chris's side, poor Lesley felt demoralized. She tried to get Chris off balance and did manage to win the first set, 6-4. Chris saw through Lesley's strategy and came back with sizzling ground strokes. She won the next two sets, 6-2, 6-3, and took the match. She became the youngest woman to reach the Forest Hills semi-finals.

Coming from behind, Chris beat Lesley Hunt at Forest Hills in 1971.

Her next opponent was Billie Jean King, three times a Wimbledon winner. Some woman players had become very jealous of Christ Evert—especially the veterans who had played for years without attracting much attention. But Billie Jean was not jealous. She thought women's tennis needed bright young stars like Chris.

"She brings out the fans," said Billie Jean. "And that's good for the game."

A huge crowd watches Chris play against Billie Jean King at Forest Hills in 1971.

Billie Jean had mixed feelings about playing against Chris. She had lost Wimbledon that year to another teenager, Evonne Goolagong of Australia. If young Chris whipped Billie Jean, people would call the older woman a has-been.

Billie Jean headed a brand-new women's pro tennis tour. She was its leader and its star. If she was defeated, her tour would probably go broke.

Billie Jean just *had* to win.

Chris returns one of King's shots during the 1971 Forest Hills semi-final.

Chris knew nothing of the turmoil in the older woman's mind. She was so cool on the court that people had nicknamed her "The Ice Princess."

Billie Jean charged out and took a quick lead, but Chris came back from 0-40 and won the first game. The crowd, all on Chris's side, screamed with happiness.

Billie Jean had not been ranked No. 1 for nothing. She unpacked her entire bag of tricks. In the seventh game of the first set, Chris double-faulted. Billie Jean broke Chris's service and won the set, 6-3.

In the second set, Billie Jean kept Chris off balance. All of Chris's shots went deep, but Billie Jean varied hers. She never let up.

The crowd warmed to the 27-year-old former champion. Billie Jean played brilliantly, and her experience was too much for young Chris.

As the 13,000 fans cheered, Billie Jean King routed Chris Evert, 6-2, and won the semi-finals.

Later, Billie Jean beat Rosie Casals for her second Forest Hills championship. Even though Chris had lost, wise tennis people knew that she would return to haunt the veterans in years to come.

Chris practices with her younger sister, Jeanne *(left),* early in 1972. Jeanne has won many tournaments and is a fine player in her own right.

Evonne Goolagong and Chris are the center of attention as they enter the court at Wimbledon in 1972.

Chris went home to Fort Lauderdale and her schoolwork. Her father would not permit her to burn herself out on the tour circuit. She still had a lot to learn.

For five months, Chris practiced and studied. She also grew taller and stronger. When she next played, in February 1972, she was better than ever. She beat Billie Jean King, 6-1, 6-0, in the Women's International Tournament. Then she began to prepare for the greatest tennis challenge of all:

Wimbledon.

A typical expression of grim concentration tightens Chris's face as she plays at Wimbledon.

The two young stars, Chris Evert and Evonne Goolagong, attracted the most attention at Wimbledon in 1972. Both women advanced to the semi-finals, where they met in a "dream match" that had the fans wild with excitement.

Chris played with precision, but Goolagong played with brilliance. Chris won the first set, 6-4, but Evonne took the next two, 6-3, 6-4.

Chris was not dismayed. She said: "I'm very satisfied with my first Wimbledon and, in a way, relieved. The next time I play Evonne, the pressure will be on *her*."

Goolagong and Evert shake hands after their Wimbledon match in 1972. Billie Jean King beat Evonne in the finals.

Chris meets some young admirers before a match in Cleveland.

A few weeks later, she had her chance. Chris played in the Bonne Bell Cup Matches that pitted American women against Australians. The pony-tailed blonde from Florida beat both Margaret Court and Evonne Goolagong to win the Cup for the United States.

This time, the tawny Goolagong seemed to have lost her powers of concentration. Chris was relentless. Eyes narrowed, concentrating utterly on the path of the ball, Chris was Little Miss Cool. She whacked the ball with her patented two-handed stroke—often grunting with the force of the blow. And she won.

Chris had been trained on a clay court and played her best games on this surface. Clay was called "slow" by expert players and favored the kind of baseline game that Chris used.

In August 1972, Chris played in the National Clay Court Tournament. She went to the finals and faced Evonne Goolagong again. She came from behind to win the first set, 7-6, then easily took the second set, 6-1. It was her first Clay Courts title. She was destined to win this tournament so often that people would say: "Chris Evert owns the Clay Courts title."

In August 1972, Chris won her first Clay Courts title against Evonne Goolagong.

But Wimbledon was a grass court—and so was Forest Hills! Grass was called "fast." This surface favored an attacking player, a woman who was not afraid to rush the net.

Chris still had problems with grass when she went to Forest Hills in 1972. She advanced to the semi-finals, but there she seemed to fall apart. Playing Australia's Kerry Melville, she served poorly. She never achieved expert baseline play, her trademark. Chris lost badly to Melville, 6-4, 6-2.

At Forest Hills in 1972, Chris lost to Kerry Melville in straight sets.

Chris Evert has always been coached by her father, Jimmy.

Chris was approaching her 18th birthday. At that time, she could turn pro. She had to decide which women's pro circuit to join. One of them was dominated by the U.S. Lawn Tennis Association. If Chris joined, she would play in tournaments with small purses, but she would be eligible for Wimbledon and Forest Hills.

The other tournament circuit was headed by Billie Jean King. It offered larger prizes. But the USLTA had banned its players from major tournaments because they were rebels. Chris decided to play for the USLTA circuit. Billie Jean and her group criticized Chris. "We are fighting for the rights of women players to earn as much money as men," said Billie Jean. "Chris should back us up."

But Chris said: "Billie Jean and the others have already won big tournaments. I haven't, and I want my chance."

Chris won $10,000 in her first pro tournament in 1973. She went on to dominate the USLTA pro circuit that season. The other star of the tour was Goolagong. People called the tour the "Ev and Chrissie Show" because the two young women were the only top players competing on it.

The tougher, more experienced players stuck with Billie Jean King. And at last the USLTA lifted its ban against the rebels. The two pro tours would merge in 1974, and King and the others were allowed to compete in major tournaments.

That was too bad for Chris. She lost four European tourneys in a row to older players.

Margaret Court defeated Chris in the 1973 French Open, 6-7, 7-6, 6-4.

At Wimbledon, Chris was able to defeat Court in the semi-finals.

Chris went to Wimbledon again. She played well during the early rounds and advanced to the semi-finals. There she played against Margaret Court, who had whipped Chris earlier in the French Open.

This time, Chris was able to dominate the tall Australian. She won, 6-1, 1-6, 6-1. Watching on the sidelines was Chris's new boy friend. He was a tennis player, too—third-ranked male in the United States. His name was Jimmy Connors.

Chris and Billie Jean King wait for the rain to stop so they can play the 1973 Wimbledon finals.

In the finals, Chris was up against Billie Jean King, who was defending her title. There was great suspense when rain interrupted the match. Chris felt the tension and it affected her game.

She was no longer the darling of the crowd. People were once again cheering for Billie Jean, who had won a tough fight against stodgy forces of the tennis "establishment." Billie Jean had become a heroine of women's liberation. Chris, who had declined to enter the fight, was called a little girl who still had a lot to learn.

Billie Jean taught her a few things at Wimbledon in 1973. King won the finals, 6-0, 7-5.

Chris kept her good humor. She said: "My father always says to hang in there, keep going. He's right and I know it. I can get better. Billie Jean and those guys, well, they're almost 30 now, aren't they? Someday it will be my turn."

She went back to America, where she said she felt more at ease, and won several minor tourneys. Then she took her second Clay Courts title. She helped the United States win the Wightman Cup again.

Her next big test was Forest Hills.

Still smiling, defeated Chris goes home from England after the 1973 Wimbledon.

In bad-luck Forest Hills semis, Chris hits one into the net, then lowers her head in dismay after the poor shot.

Before Forest Hills, Chris told a reporter: "I'm not used to losing. This year's European tour was proof that I could. It made me realize that I wasn't putting 100 per cent into my matches. I wasn't hungry enough to win!"

Chris tries to look brave as Margaret Court gives her a consoling pat on the shoulder. It was Chris's third straight loss in the Forest Hills semis.

She made a hard fight of it at Forest Hills, but she still wasn't ready to win a big one on grass. After reaching the semis, she went down before Margaret Court, 7-5, 2-6, 6-2. It was her third straight loss in the Forest Hills semis.

Chris and Jimmy Connors became engaged late in 1973. She began to talk about romance and her love of family life. "I'm basically a homebody," she said. "I'd like to keep house and have two to four children. Tennis is not the center of my life any more."

She and Jimmy were an attractive couple. And they played good tennis, too. Chris worked hard to improve her serve, which had been weak. She lost weight and began to run faster.

Chris Evert and Jimmy Connors

Chris and her mother, Colette, get ready for a costume pageant that preceded the 1974 Family Circle Magazine tournament. Chris's gown represents the latest thing in ladies' tennis garb in 1874.

In 1974, Chris finally reached top form. She was no longer afraid to rush the net and her serve had at last become a weapon.

She won the Italian Open, her first major international title. Not only did she win the singles, against Martina Navratilova of Czechoslovakia, but she also won the doubles. She teamed up with Russian Olga Morozova, her friend.

Two weeks later, Chris beat Olga for the French singles championship. She and Olga teamed up to win the French doubles.

Once again, it was time for Wimbledon.

Chris in action against Morozova during the 1974 Wimbledon.

In an early match, Chris had a bad scare. She played Lesley Hunt of Australia to a 9-9 tie in the third set. Then the match was postponed because of darkness.

Early next morning, Chris practiced with Jimmy Connors. When her match with Hunt took up again, Chris broke the Australian's service and won, 8-6, 5-7, 11-9.

After that, it was smooth sailing to the finals, where she was to meet her Russian friend, Olga Morozova.

Chris was confident now. Not only was she the master of the baseline game, but she also showed her power with excellent volleying and a good overhead game.

Chris beat the Russian woman with ease, 6-0, 6-4, wearing her down and waiting for her to make mistakes. When it was all over, Chris tossed her racket joyfully into the air. Olga gave her a kiss on the cheek. It was Chris's 36th victory in a row—the most important one of all in the tennis world.

The Wimbledon title hers at last, Chris throws her racket high into the air.

Jimmy Connors had cheered her victory. Now it became her turn to cheer his. He reached the semis after a tough battle, then whipped Dick Stockton in four sets. In the finals, he defeated veteran Ken Rosewall easily.

Chris and Jimmy posed with their Wimbledon trophies in what was called the "tennis love match" of the century.

By December, when Chris had earned a record-breaking $261,460, the two had decided to call the engagement off. "Some day we may get together again," Chris said. "But right now there isn't room for anything in our lives but tennis."

His and hers Wimbledon trophies gleam as Jimmy Connors kisses his fiance, Chris Evert, after their 1974 triumph.

Chris won the 1975 French Open.

Both Chris and Jimmy were now ranked No. 1 in the United States. They continued to play the game brilliantly. Once, they said that they would become engaged again—but not long afterward, they decided not to get married.

Chris said: "I'm asking questions I never asked before. I was shielded from a lot of realities about women and I accepted some roles—such as being a wife and mother—without much thought. I'm not saying I know all the answers about my future or my career—who does?—but at least I'm asking."

In 1975, Chris Evert was named Female Athlete of the Year. She was no longer a fairy tale come true, but a woman who played her game proudly and well.

She won the World Series of Women's Tennis against Billie Jean King in sudden death. At Wimbledon in 1975, King defeated Chris. That was to be Billie Jean's last major tournament, so Chris didn't mind.

Then came Forest Hills—the one big tournament that Chris had never won. In 1975, Forest Hills had a new clay surface. Chris had won 83 straight matches on clay. She was a heavy favorite.

She reached the finals, and there met Evonne Goolagong Cawley. The Australian won the first set, 7-5. In the second, she put Chris on the defensive, but Chris stayed unflappable. She stormed back to win the second set, 6-4.

Then it was Evonne's turn to feel pressure. Evonne led 1-0 and 2-1 in the third. Chris whittled away and distracted Evonne with her baseline game. She took four games in a row. Evonne faltered and Chris won the set and the match, 6-2.

"This victory is more important than my 1974 Wimbledon title," Chris Evert said. "This is my national championship. This is my home."

Chris hustles during the 1976 Wimbledon classic as she wins the semi-final match against Martina Navratilova. She went on to defeat Yvonne Goolagong Cawley of Australia.

Chris beat Cawley again in the finals of the U.S. Open on September 11, 1976. It was her second victory in a row at Forest Hills.

The 1976 season was a golden one for Chris. She won the Wimbledon crown again, but she had tough going against Evonne Goolagong Cawley of Australia. Chris won the first set, 6-3. Evonne grabbed the second, 6-4. Then both women fought for their lives. Chris went to the net and came from behind to win, 8-6.

Later that year, at Forest Hills, she repeated her triumph over Cawley. This time her score was 6-3, 6-0. With her earlier Virginia Slims Tournament win, Chris had earned the women's Triple Crown of tennis. She was elected president of the Women's Tennis Association and was hailed for earning more money than any woman athlete in history.

Chris Evert was 21 years old.

Nobody called her "Princess of Tennis" any more. She was the Queen.

Billie Jean King congratulates Chris, who won the Wimbledon quarter-finals in 1977. But in the semis that year, Chris was upset by Britain's Virginia Wade.

Chris stands in the doorway of New York's famous Madison Square Garden, where she won the 1977 Virginia Slims Championship for the fourth time.